Think Persian

Think Persian

by John Kollock

PEACHTREE PUBLISHERS, LTD.

Published by
PEACHTREE PUBLISHERS, LTD.
494 Armour Circle, N.E.
Atlanta, Georgia 30324

Copyright © 1984 John Kollock

2nd printing 1985

All Rights Reserved

Printed in the United States of America

ISBN: 0-931948-71-1

Library of Congress Catalog No. 83-051800

To Carey, who understands the needs of animals

This is not a funny animal story. There is nothing funny about being an animal.

It is also not about fuzzy creatures dressed up in human clothes and acting like them. Animals do not normally choose to dress that way. I have never met a dog or cat who asked to be stuffed into a pair of blue jeans or a peasant blouse. Some dogs do occasionally become fond of little blankets tied over their backs. But then dogs have a lot of funny ideas.

Being an animal is serious business. Being a cat is even more serious. I have been one for 16 or 17 years, and let me tell you it is not all bits of chicken and kitty litter.

In addition to being constantly compared in their actions to human behavior, cats are constantly under attack for lack of affection, too much independence, and fleas.

"Dogs," they are always saying, "Look at the dog — man's best friend." Whose best friend is a cat?

Himself.

Not even another cat, except on certain moonlit nights. The dog always wags his tail, if he has one, and most of his back end if he hasn't. Then there is all that jumping about whenever his master or mistress comes within sight. Why all the hysterics? They haven't been anywhere of importance, and nine out of ten times they don't have anything for you.

Cats do not wag their tails — under any circumstances. Fly to the moon, or go to Florida for the winter and you will get narry a wag. That sort of nervous twitch could only bring on arthritis or falling fur.

A cat may arch his tail and sway it meaningfully to and fro, which is to indicate that something dramatic is afoot, but it is always done with dignity. A cat frantically flip-flopping his endpiece would simply tell the world that he was unaware of his own heritage.

I tell you all of this because if you, dear reader, are a cat, then I need to share with you the great knowledge I have come into over the years. If you are not a cat, then it may help you to know how wonderfully wise we are. If you are a dog, then you probably can't read anyway and by now you have chewed the back off of this volume and will get punished for it.

Good.

First let me say that the world has changed vastly since I was a kit. Plastic garbage bags. That is the main source of our downfall as the last of the world's independent creatures. Time was when a cat could wander his whole life, from garbage can to garbage can dining in elegance. The tasty world of leftovers was his for the grappling. Occasionally there would be some selfish human who would clamp the lid down too tightly for our delicate claws to uncap. But this was a trifle amid the feast we had to choose from. The back fence and barn were our kingdom, and only the fat, lazy, inbred felines would subject themselves to the fuss and feathers of house life for their bowl of cream and nibbles.

Then came the plastic bag and the twist ties with which every human seems to delight in lashing up the opening.

And there you are.

Out goes the garbage on Tuesday and in no time a snorting metal monster roars up and the bags are popped into its jaws. Then whurr - scrunch - and off they go. With them goes your breakfast, lunch, dinner and party snack.

Mice, who used to be our staple food are now hunted down for sport by men in white suits with tanks of poison spray. If you down a stray titmouse or blue jay on a lawn there is always some lady around to beat you on the head with her broom before you can enjoy your dinner.

Face it, my friend, there is only one way to live in this modern world — you have to adopt a human.

Much as it goes against the nature of our independent heritage, we have to learn to at least give the appearance of being part of their strange society. True, there are days when I would rather have taken up housekeeping with a turtle or rabbit — but a cat has to eat. And it is a proven fact that humans waste more food than any other animal in the kingdom.

Choosing the right human to adopt is a very tricky business. At first glance they all look alike. It's true they come in several colors and keep changing their coverings from moment to moment, but beyond this there are subtle differences that only a creature as sensitive as a cat could appreciate. Their household habits must be noted to insure that you will want to be around them all of the time.

Do they like to bring in the right sort of bags of food, and plenty of it?

Some humans exist on nothing but rabbit food. A cat could starve waiting for a bit of tuna fish or some overcooked liver.

Other humans bounce about in rubber shoes with their bare limbs hanging out. They survive on what looks like rat pellets and liquids which are definitely not milk.

There are also those who buy only what they call "economy cat food," which has a flavor somewhere between damp cardboard and sawdust. If you turn up your nose at it, they will say you are off your feed. But you don't see them having it for dinner first and offering you the leftovers.

11

Even after you have selected a good provider, there are many little bits of wisdom which you will need to know about handling the average human pet so that your world will run smoothly.

In order to explain all of this I must share with you some of my personal history. I could say that I do this with great modesty — but I don't. I am proud of the fact that I have survived for so long in a household which is far from average.

My name is Cricket. It is not the sort of name I would have chosen. I would have preferred Lawrence. You don't call a Lawrence to come and eat up a bit of bacon that has fallen under the table — you request. I have met a lot of Puffys and Fluffies and Mewmews, but never a Lawrence. Pity.

Before I became Cricket I was not referred to at all in the singular. We were "the kittens," or more often as "those cats." Mother was an aristocrat from Charleston, and none of her family had been north of Meeting Street for five generations. However, during the heat of summer she would travel in a large wicker basket to her country home in the mountains accompanied by her faithful human pets.

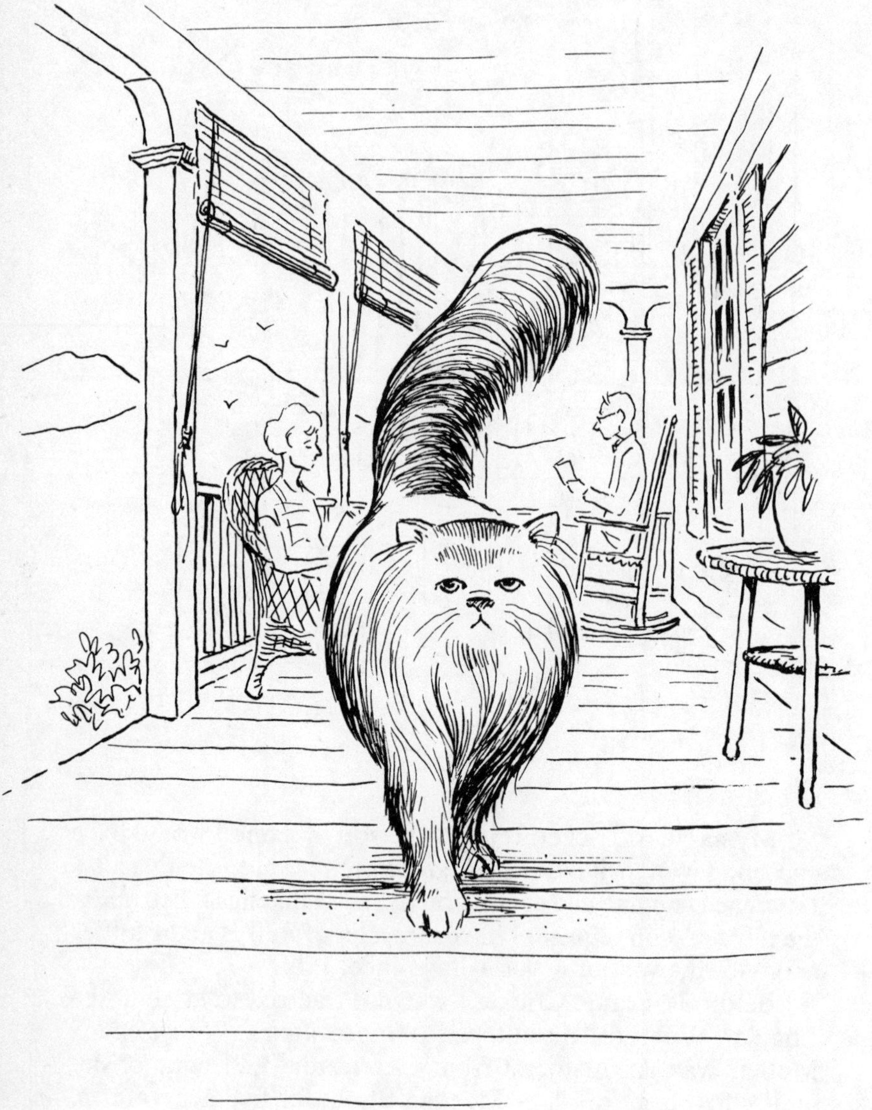

My earliest memories of Mumz were of her walking with stately dignity the length of the front piazza, casting never an eye to butterfly or bird as she aired her fur.

My father was a local cat who worked in the crossroads store down at the end of the lane. I was told that sometimes he would prance on his hind legs when the mountain humans played clogging music on Saturday night. At any rate he must have had some charm or Mumz would have never let him on the piazza.

My nearest kin were a mixed litter who were born along with myself under the bottom step just inside the drip line of summer rains.

Mumz called me "Mew." At least that was all she *ever* called me. In fact, that was all she ever called any of us.

For all of her breeding, she was not exactly a devoted mother. I think she really regarded us as a moment of summer madness that would have never been understood in Charleston.

When Labor Day came she crawled under the step for one last moment of advice on how we should face the world as we grew to cathood. Looking each of us in the face she seemed to recognize that we were different, even if she had never bothered to find out which was which.

"Mew," she said with her slightly low country accent. Each of us took this to be a specific greeting to ourself. It was a tender moment. She seemed to have difficulty accepting the fact that this collection of grey, yellow and ringtailed kittens was a part of her. Finally she said with a sigh —

"You may never look like much, but always remember — think Persian."

It was good advice. Even after I had grown into a large, rawboned, black and white, somewhat average looking alley cat on the outside — I knew deep within I was Persian.

Mumz and her wicker basket disappeared in a cloud of gasoline fumes and red clay dust. After an afternoon of playing stalk-the-tail in the burnt out summer grass, my family split up.

That fall I knew the joy and occasional inconvenience of being my own cat. I roamed the countryside and ate native game and farmhouse garbage. I met a few casual lady cats and fought some Toms for sport and exercise.

Fall in the mountains is full of long, lazy warm days, just right for napping. Being in my first year I didn't know that just after fall comes winter.

Winter is not designed for cats. It gets too wet and cold. The fresh food flies away or goes deep in the ground.

As the weather continued to grow more unpleasant, I wandered the soggy woodlands in search of those warm days I had become accustomed to. I found nothing but dead leaves and an occasional rock shelter to make my bed under.

Then one day the smell of burning pine and oak drifted through the trees. I explored its source. It led to a farmhouse. On approaching one of the windows, I made a discovery. For all of their bumbling ways, humans did know how to live in cold weather. Lack of fur had somehow made them clever enough to discover such delightful things as fire, hot food and the afghan coverlet.

For the first time I was tempted to adopt a pet human.

Then chance prevented me from making a selection.

It happened one day as I was exploring a rambling assortment of little sheds surrounding a large building that seemed to be uncertain as to whether it wanted to be a house or a barn. It wandered off in several directions with no apparent purpose. Parts of it were painted and other sections were not. No two windows were the same size and the doors were equally mis-matched. I was, of course, no authority on human houses, but my instinct told me that I would find this one less than cozy even if there was a fire going inside.

There was none at the moment.

There also were no signs of casually discarded nibbles in the garbage cans. I had made my breakfast on a very lean field mouse and there seemed no prospect for supper here. I was about to head down the little dirt road which ran in front of the building, when suddenly the way was blocked by a rattling old car filled with chattering humans.

I ducked into the shelter of one of the sheds and watched as two big humans and three smaller ones tumbled out of the car armed with saws and axes. After a little chatter and pointing they began to rush around hacking bits of tree limbs and berry bushes. These they shoved into the old car.

Then it happened.

My fate was sealed by one of the larger small humans shouting — "A kitten. Look, a darling kitten."

By this time in my life I had come to regard myself as a mature and complete cat. Such references as "kittie" and "kitten" were from my past.

I sniffed indignantly and prepared to make a break for the woods, but I had not counted on the swiftness of small humans, particularly the smallest one who had me by the tail, forepaw and tummy all at once in one swift lunge.

The next thing I knew I was being clutched and fondled by an assortment of hands, none of which let me go. The humans were all talking at once, which is the strange way they have of communicating. Suddenly to my horror they plopped me, along with the bits of greenery, into the old car.

I heard scraps of conversation through the glass about keeping me as a Christmas present and how sweet I was. This was not true, then or now. I am my own cat. Agreeable I may be — but never sweet.

I decided to hide as far under the front seat as I could get, in hopes that they would forget about me. Later I could escape.

After a while they all piled into the car, and before I could untangle myself from the old rags and candy wrappers, the car was rumbling and snorting off down the road.

How long did we travel? Very long. I think I even napped a bit, although I promised myself that I would remain alert so that when the humans finally stopped and got out — which I assumed they would eventually do — I would make one giant leap and be off into the woods again.

No such luck.

When we finally stopped, my path was immediately blocked by many hands, each trying to catch hold of some part of me to pull. Then the largest human got most of me in his grip and the others let go.

I was too confused to realize where I was until I found myself inside a warm dry house filled with light. The humans trooped into a room where there were rather more good smells than usual. Suddenly I was dumped in front of a bowl of fresh milk.

"Eat, Kittie," said the next to the smallest human.

Now panic is one thing — and being squeezed or pulled is one thing — and being called "kittie" when you are a full grown cat is one thing — but fresh milk, especially after a long day with only one skinny mouse for breakfast, is enough to make all of those other things unimportant.

I "ate" my milk.

Then I ate some tuna and a little chicken. Then I drank some more milk. Then I had a tad of liver and a little more chicken. Then I began to feel quite sleepy.

All around me a ring of humans quietly watched me fill up. I ignored them. "Soon," I told myself, "I will make my escape and be back in the woods." I began to stagger a bit from the weight of the food I had inhaled. One of the humans scooped me up. "If you squeeze me now," I thought, "I will explode and there will be bits of me all over this room."

But the human didn't squeeze, and the next thing I knew it was like summer again. I was in a box full of soft warm rags. "I will rest a little," I told myself, "and then I will spring off into the woods."

That was the last thing I remembered.

When I awoke there was a small human face right next to mine.

"Hello, Cricket," said the human. And that, my cats, was all I had to say about who I became.

I woke to a world that I knew nothing about. Outside the human houses were everywhere. There were no fields. No dirt lanes. Instead there were hard black streets and neat patches of grass. There were neat patches of flowers and neat patches of bushes. There were no barns or deep woods. There were trees, but not many. Mostly there were houses, and humans, and cars, and plastic garbage bags.

When the humans who had captured me finally let me out for a walk, I soon decided that the safest place to be was inside the house where there was always a good supply of food.

So that was how I came to adopt a family of human pets.

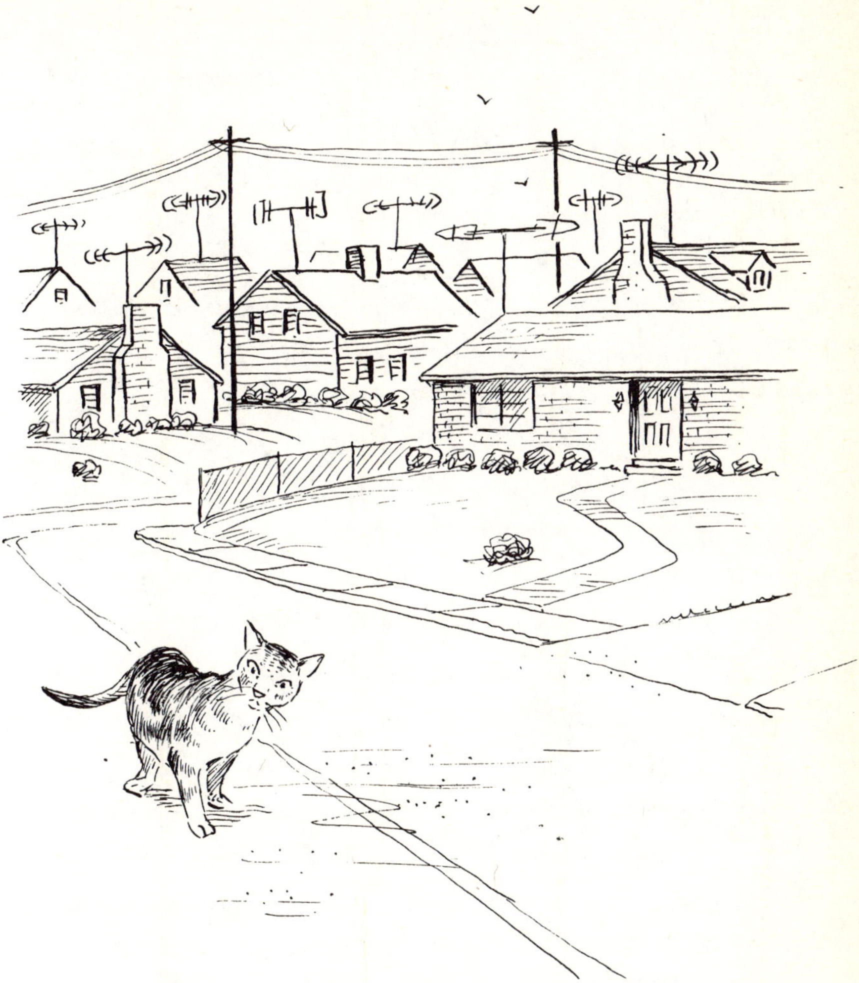

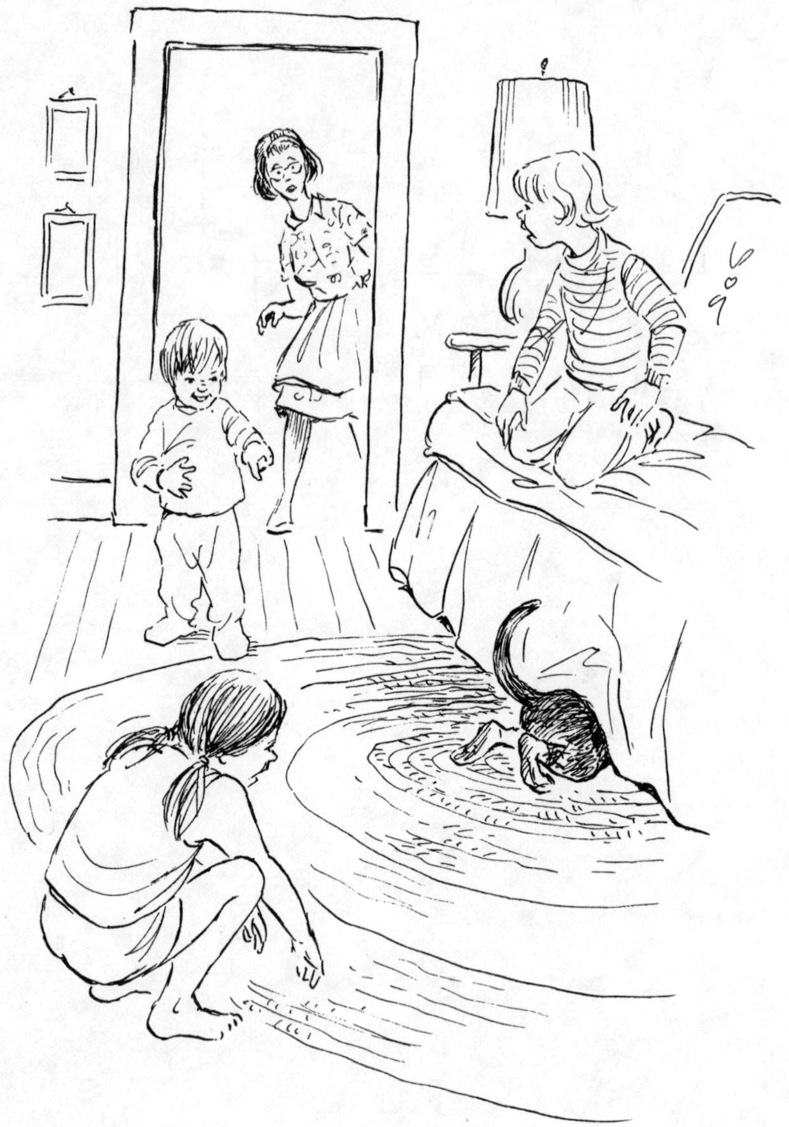

I think in some strange way they had decided that it was really *they* who had done the adopting. It never occurred to them that all I had to do was walk away. However, if you will take my advice, this is the best way to leave it. Humans are much more ready with the good pleasures of life if they think the whole thing is their idea. A good human pet should at least assume that he is in command.

Which brings me to the task of informing you as to the method of training your new human pet.

First of all, next to food and a soft bed, there is the matter of house breaking. Humans are easy to train. This simple procedure usually works.

When you arrive in your new home, wander about in a vague way, as if you are looking for something. A slight look of confused urgency will help. Make your way toward the best rug or duck under some low furniture.

Almost like magic the humans will appear with either a simple sand box or one of the more elaborate sports models complete with interesting smelling materials.

Once broken to the habit, a human seems never to forget. Or if they do, a tastefully placed wet spot in the entrance hall or on the nighttime path to the bathroom will jog their memory.

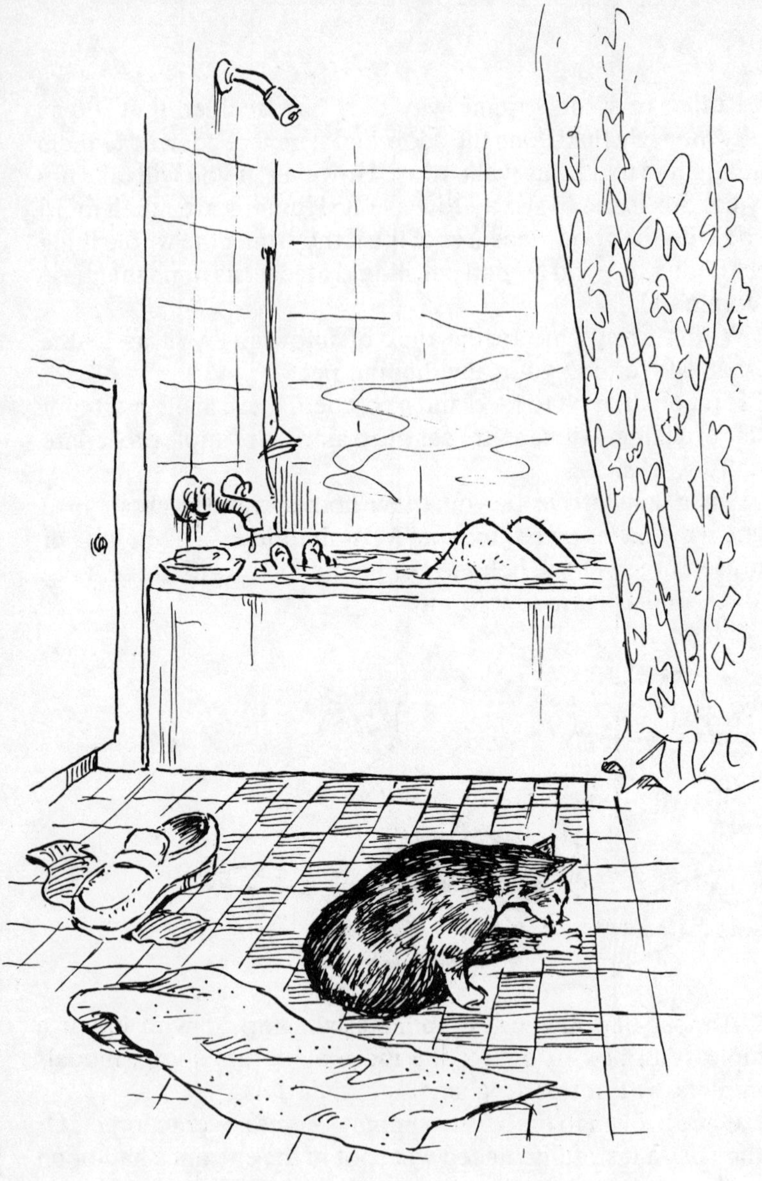

Humans are generally neat creatures. They do not wash as often — or as well — as we cats do, but they make much more fuss over the procedure. Instead of lying in the sun and leisurely backlicking themselves, the average human will plunge into a shallow house pond or find a rainstorm in the closet to splutter and gasp under. Of the two, the pond sitter seems to be the happier. Sometimes they will lie deep in the water with only their head and bits of this and that showing above the surface. For some reason, the colder the weather, the hotter the pond gets. The heat turns the human quite red which seems to please them.

Occasionally small humans think it would be fun for us cats to wash in this manner. It is not. I would suggest that you make it painfully clear that we know far more about how to wash ourselves than they do. Scratch, if necessary, but not too deeply.

While I am on the subject of human characteristics, I think it would be good to go into some of the peculiar traits you will run into. You see, not all humans react the same, and some do not even recognize how honored they should feel at being adopted by a cat. How anyone could not love a cat is beyond me. But then humans are a lot like dogs — very unpredictable. Perhaps this is the reason they are "best friends."

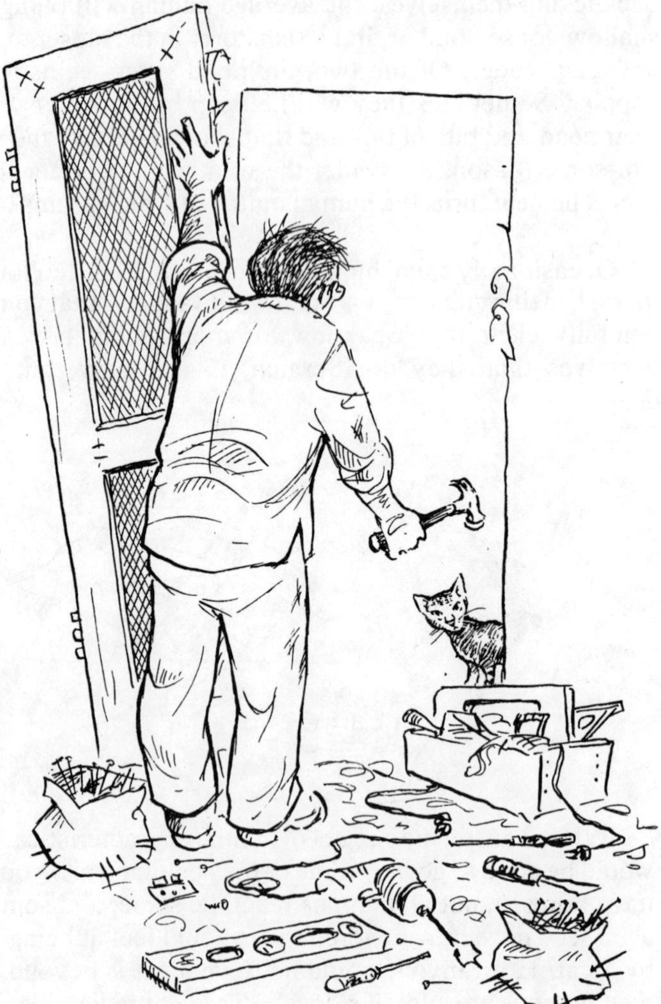

To begin with, you must learn to tell the difference between the male and female human. The physical characteristics are similar to those of cats. Here the distinction ends.

Be warned.

The male human has much less taste and appreciation of subtle things. He is likely to react to the natural act of our curling up on his head for warmth on a cold night in a violent manner. Cats have been known to sail out open windows as a reaction to this simple move.

My own experience with the humans I adopted was very much along these lines. The only male human in my house spent most of the day somewhere else.

At least at first.

Other humans who came visiting kept calling him Artist, although I don't think that was his name. When he was in the house he usually wore baggy old clothes covered with smears of color. I have always thought of him as Old Paint.

Male humans are often very noisy. Old Paint was even more so. He was always banging on something or painting it another color. I had to keep on the alert to avoid getting tacky paws or badly discolored fur if I wanted to rub a door casing or table leg.

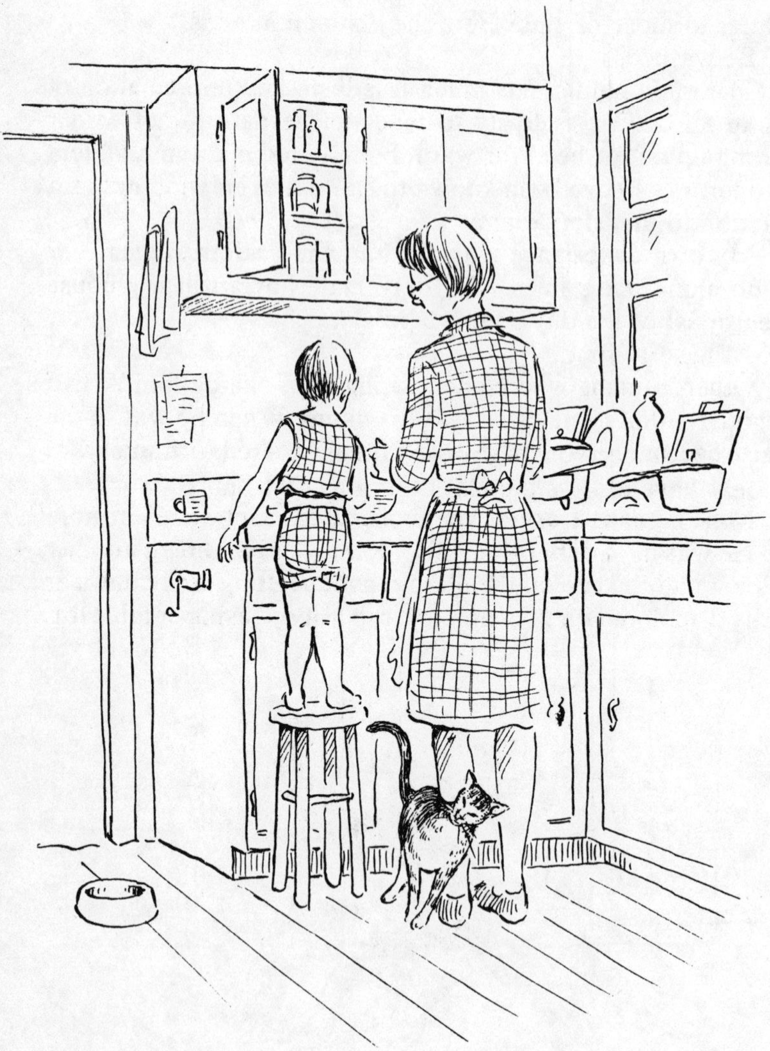

The other humans in my house were female. They are your greatest allies. They are much more sensitive to your needs and seem to understand the complex nature of cats. It is my opinion that the female human is the more intelligent and therefore the more easily trained.

In a very short time they will come to understand that you want to be fed if you simply rub their legs with your shoulders and backsides.

Male humans, on the other hand, quite often refuse to learn this simple command and react by kicking you across the kitchen.

Patience is necessary in these cases and the act should be repeated as often as possible in hope that eventually they will pick up the message.

However, in the interest of time it is always easier to approach the female. Obviously she responds to kindness better and seems to gain great satisfaction in stroking our spinal cords. She also loves to hear us purr. Never hold back on giving the female your best and loudest purr when she does something right. Her next move is always to do something to please you.

My own personal large female human pet was perhaps the best bit of luck I ever came into. The name she was trained to come to is Nancy. To me she has always been Sweet Nancy, because she has never failed to learn new tricks and always seems to desire to please me with everything from tid-bits to long hours of lap service. Next to sunshine, Sweet Nancy is my most dependable friend.

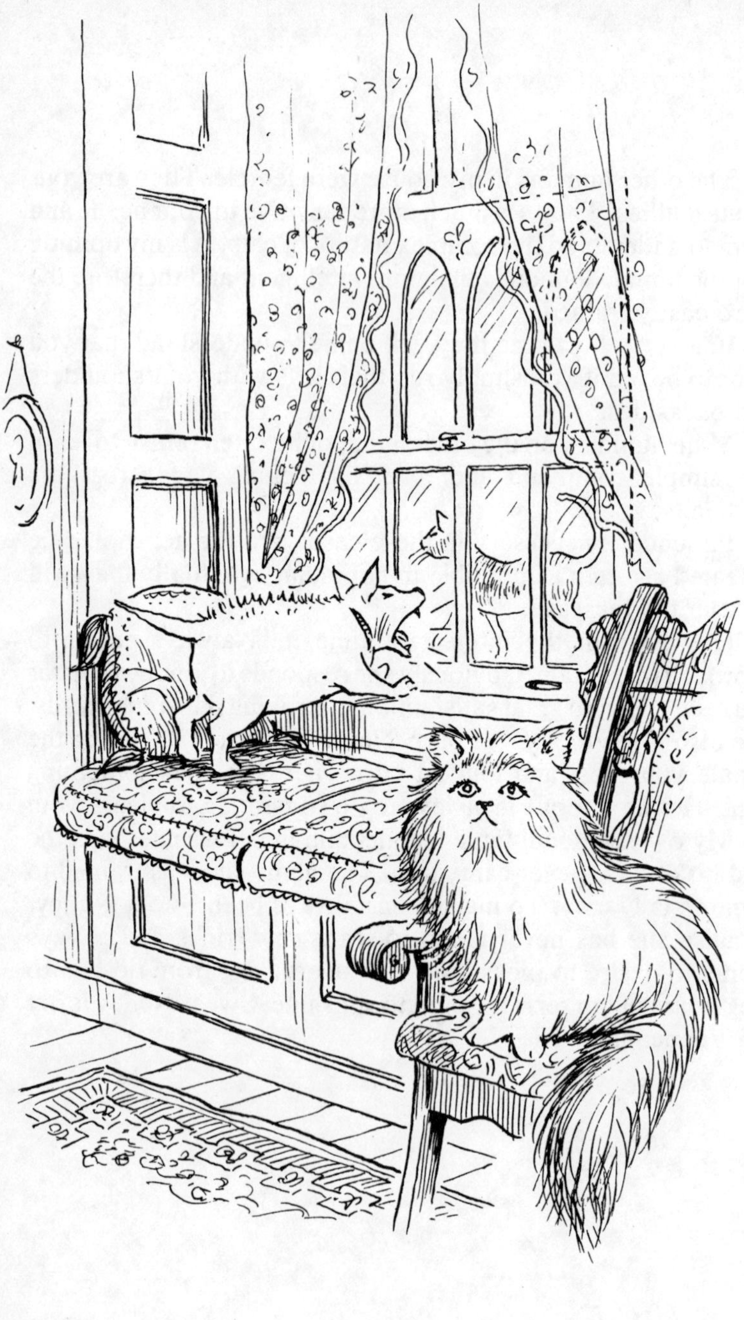

There are, of course, many variations in female humans. Other cats I have known have told me about some of them.

There are those who lavish almost too much affection on us and in return expect us never to leave the house. I personally don't know how a cat can live without a bit of roaming.

Usually housebound cats are hung up on their family history and spend a lot of time tracing their line back to show how pure they are. "Great-great-grandfather was a Siamese, and his grandmother was descended from the first family to come to Savannah . . ." You know the type. They sit on their velvet tuffets and drink pure cream until their fur begins to go bad and then they have to go to the vet for treatments.

One cat I knew named Fluffy Scarlet never left her home in a large Victorian house. She would stroll from her bedroom on the second floor down to the dining room at meal times. There was a dog that stayed inside all of the time, too. His name was Snarley-boo. He was badly overweight, yet in typical dogginess he felt it was necessary to go into hysterical barking fits if anyone came past the large bay window.

On my daily ramble I used to find some entertainment in walking the ledge outside the window to drive him into apoplexy. When he would finally collapse into a wheezing spell on the floor, I would talk with Fluffy Scarlet about her confined existence.

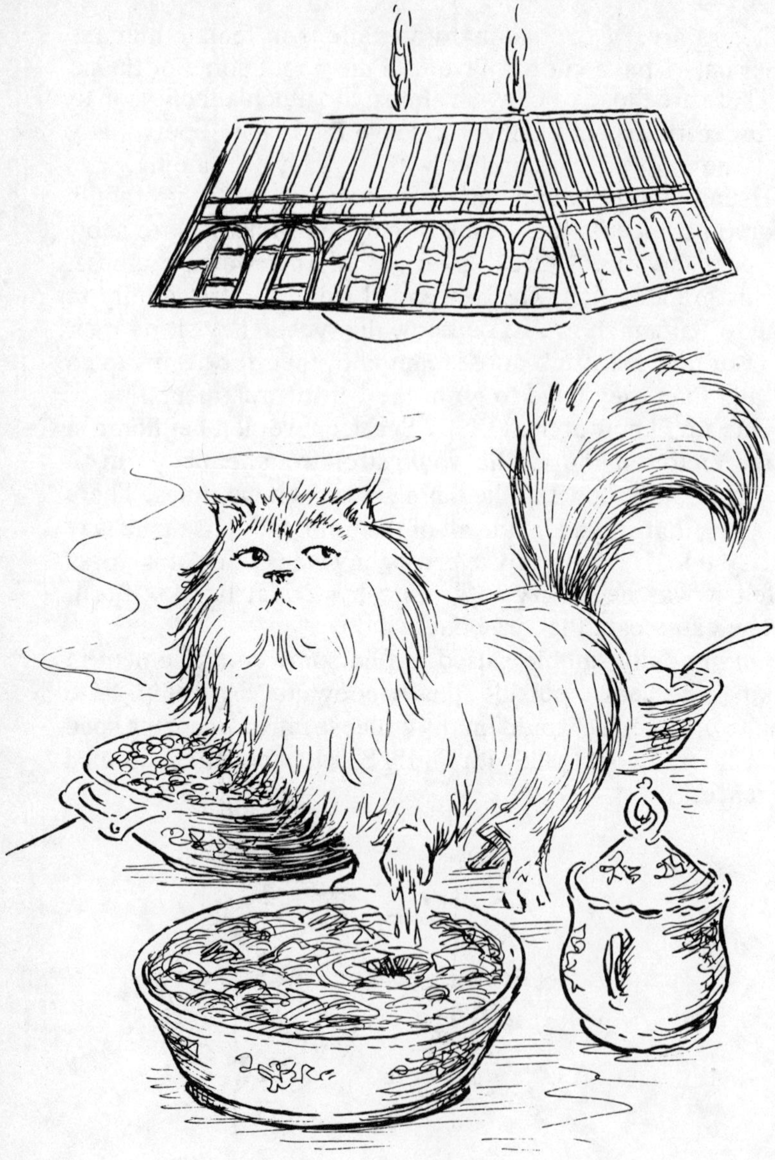

She was quite chatty, although I doubt that she would have ever considered me her equal. It seemed she had a very interesting way of entertaining herself.

At human mealtime she would land on the table and walk slowly down the center, inspecting the bowls of food. The humans, being very well trained, never disturbed the ritual. If there was something that Fluffy Scarlet particularly craved for her dinner, she would accidentally step in the bowl and then flick her foot to make sure the humans had seen the action. Without fail the humans would avoid taking any of that food, so there would be plenty for Fluffy Scarlet when her mealtime came. Even human visitors at the table seemed to learn very quickly to avoid her selections — which shows that they really can learn if you are patient.

My own life was never so easy. I tried the table bit once or twice, but even Sweet Nancy would always carefully put me on the floor before I could make a choice. Old Paint was even less perceptive and often backhanded me into the living room.

I finally gave up on trying to teach them this trick.

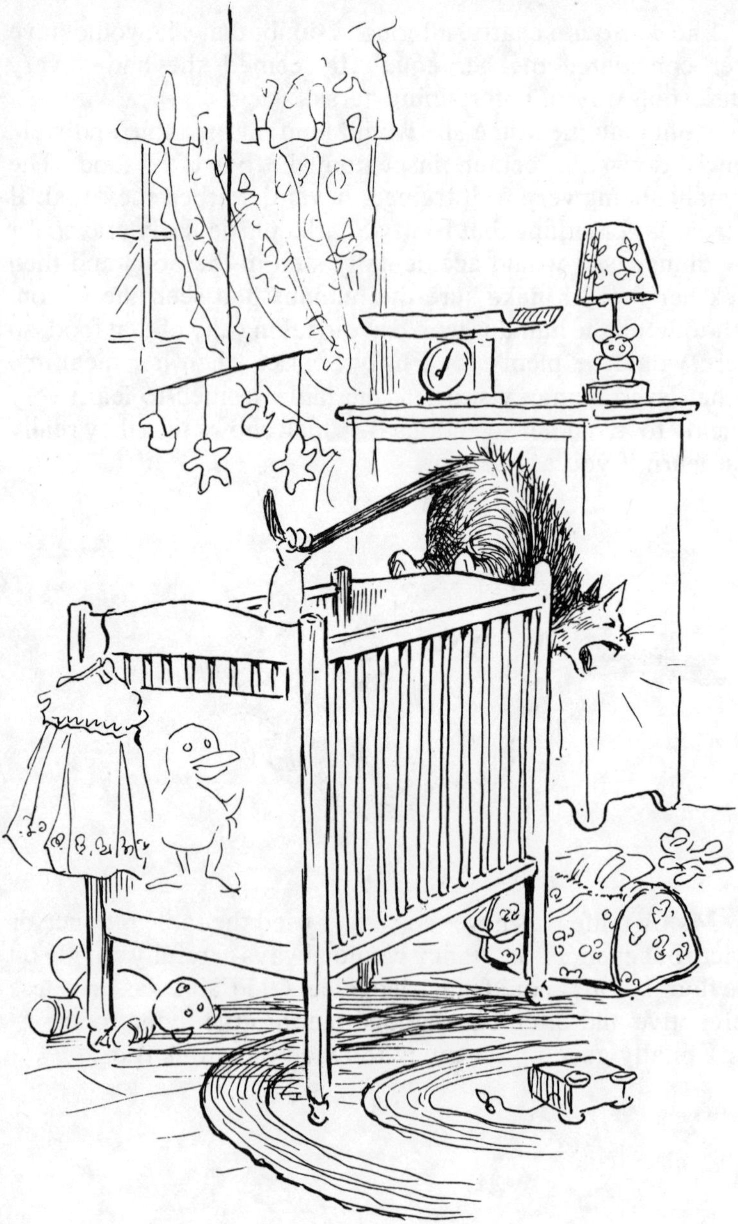

I haven't told you yet about the smaller human pets that come with many houses. Like kittens, they eventually grow into large humans and go away, but it takes much longer. I suppose this is because they are very slow to learn the natural habits that the female humans try to teach them.

They get their eyes open quite soon after they are born, but instead of beginning to bounce about and chase their tails, it is sometimes years before they can do more than loll around and make terrible noises before and after they are fed.

Do not get too close to them at this early age. They are curious about us and have unusual strength. If they get hold of your tail it is possible for you to get a very bad strain from their yanking before someone comes to release you.

The female human is also very protective of her young. They have been known to speak as harshly as the male if you try to lick the excess milk off a messy little human.

In my household I had no very small humans when I adopted them. They were all able to walk on their hind feet in that curious way humans do.

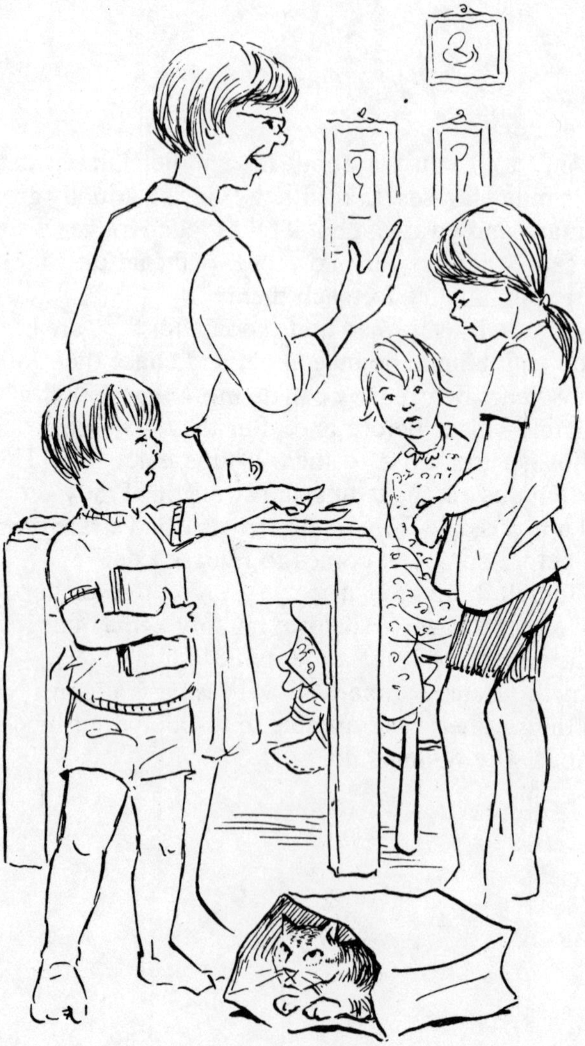

The smallest one spoke only in short direct phrases, which I much prefer. Humans spend a great deal of time using their voices to confuse and upset each other. Then they spend even more time explaining and making up. In between, they chatter endlessly about things that have no meaning for me.

Sweet Nancy even spends a long time each day talking to a box that makes a ringing noise when it wants to be talked to. I do not think the box is part of the human kingdom, but they all seem to be very fond of it. Each of them spends some time chattering about nothing to the thing. Sweet Nancy chatters the most, but then she is so kind that perhaps she feels it is lonesome and needs her attention. It is really a shame that we cannot teach humans to purr more and talk less. It would be so much more peaceful.

My smallest human pet was called Meg. For some years I had to be very careful of Meg because she was never very respectful of how she picked me up.

Cats, as we all know, are quite flexible and can, by choice, bend in many supple directions. However, a death grip by the midsection with one's head hanging down is not my favorite way to travel.

Meg loved to pounce on me at unexpected moments. I have always tried to be patient in dealing with small humans. I know some cats say "Spare-the-claw-and-spoil-the-human," but I try to be tolerant and only raise my voice into a yowl when physical danger is apparent.

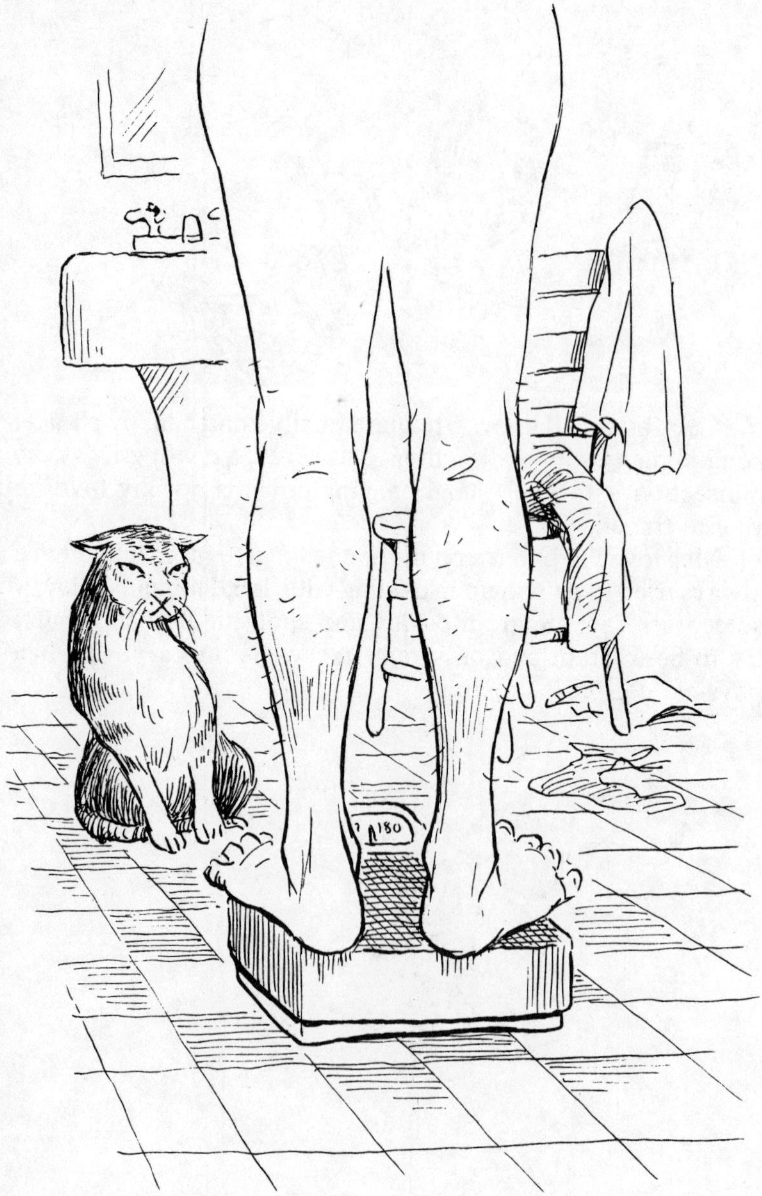
180

I mentioned earlier that animals do not like to dress up in human coverings. I understand in the case of humans that a lack of fur has forced them to hang things over their heads or step into hind leg covers and cinch them to their middles with straps and strings. Also, humans, without these coverings are rather pitiful looking. Occasionally I have been trapped in the little rooms where they wash themselves. There they will stand about briefly as they came into the world. They are quite sad looking. Rather a pale pink like newborn rats, with not enough fur to keep them through one cold night on the front steps. I could go on, but it is really too distasteful for me to discuss. Suffice it to say that humans really *do* need clothes.

Cats do not.

However, small humans seem to think otherwise. It may be the bad influence of the books they look at. For some reason, beyond my understanding, the books always seem to depict animals dressed in human outfits, looking quite proud and happy with themselves.

They are also shown living in smaller versions of human houses. I don't know how they are supposed to get these houses since humans do not seem inclined to build them, and certainly I have never known a cat — no matter how gifted — who took naturally to a hammer and saw.

Occasionally little humans will have small houses in their possessions, but I have never found them very appealing except for an occasional nap.

More than once, I am sad to say, Meg and her friends forced me into outlandish getups. Thus inhibited from rushing off to the nearest tree, I have been forced to endure tea parties made up of gooey chocolate things and sticky sweet drinks which they attempted to pour down my throat while making human chit-chat.

All I can give you in the way of advice is to run when you see them starting to play dress-up. In a few years they will give up this unnatural pursuit and allow you to wear only the fur you came in.

I had very little trouble in training my other two small humans. Kathleen, the next largest, was given to taking long naps when I first arrived. I thought she might be part cat at first. It was a great comfort to me to find a human so sensible in her habits.

We could spend long afternoons on the big human's bed, sleeping and purring. Late in the day Old Paint would come bumbling in. If he did not immediately begin banging and sawing, he might crash into the bed and nap also. He seemed to enjoy having Kathleen for company, but he was far less generous with me.

Within a few years Kathleen began disappearing for a time during the day, along with the biggest little human who was called Carey. When she came in after lunch, instead of settling down for a nap she would go into the living room and try to stand on her head.

"She is trying to learn to stand on her head," Sweet Nancy would explain.

This seemed obvious. But *why* was not so clear. Humans look silly enough standing on their hind legs. But a human standing on her head is perfectly useless. She didn't even serve as a good scratching post. The moment I got a good claw hold, she shrieked and fell in a lump on the floor.

Once Kathleen had perfected staying on her head for several minutes at a time, she stopped doing it.

"Now," I heard Sweet Nancy tell a visitor, "Kathleen is learning to ride a bike."

Another useless pursuit, with the added danger of my tail occasionally getting squashed. But for all of her strange activities I must say that Kathleen never once tried to pour sticky-sweet down my throat or make me wear Raggedy Andy hand-me-downs.

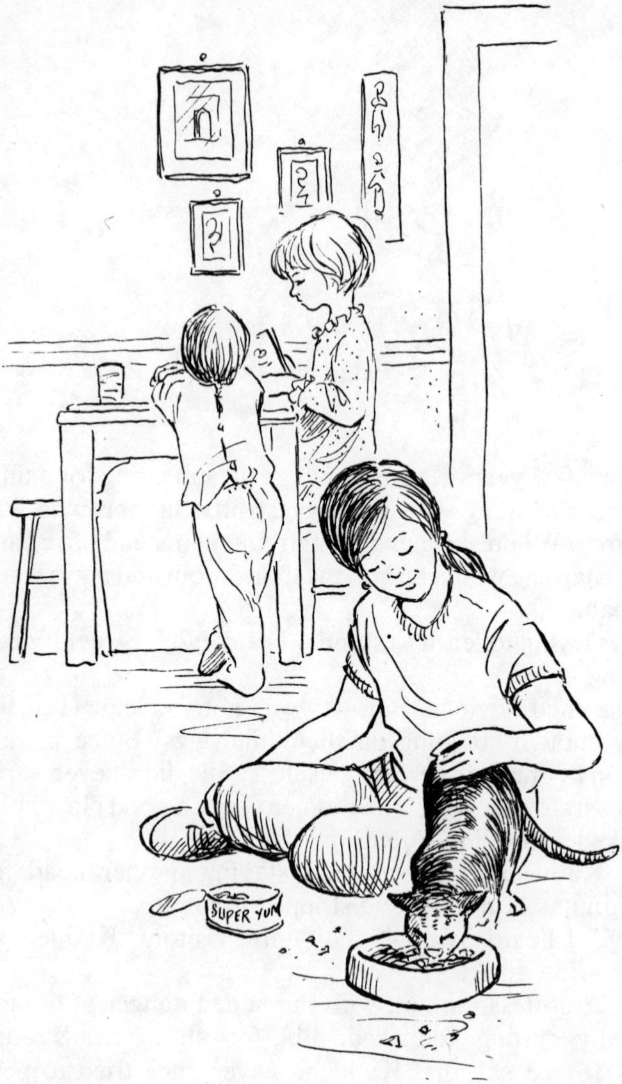
SUPER YUM

Carey, the biggest little human, was a love. Next to Sweet Nancy, she was my best pet. In no time I had her trained to feed me on command. As she grew older she could also tell when they were trying to slip inferior cat food into my rations.

"Cricket doesn't like that dry stuff," she would announce. She would be right.

"Cricket needs more blankets in her basket," she would mention as the weather got colder. Soon bits of old flannel nightgowns or shreds of Old Paint's worn clothes would find their way into my bedding. Always appreciated.

When Carey was small she was too busy to sit still for long. But when she got bigger, her lap was available for hours at a time. Especially during afternoon soap time on TV.

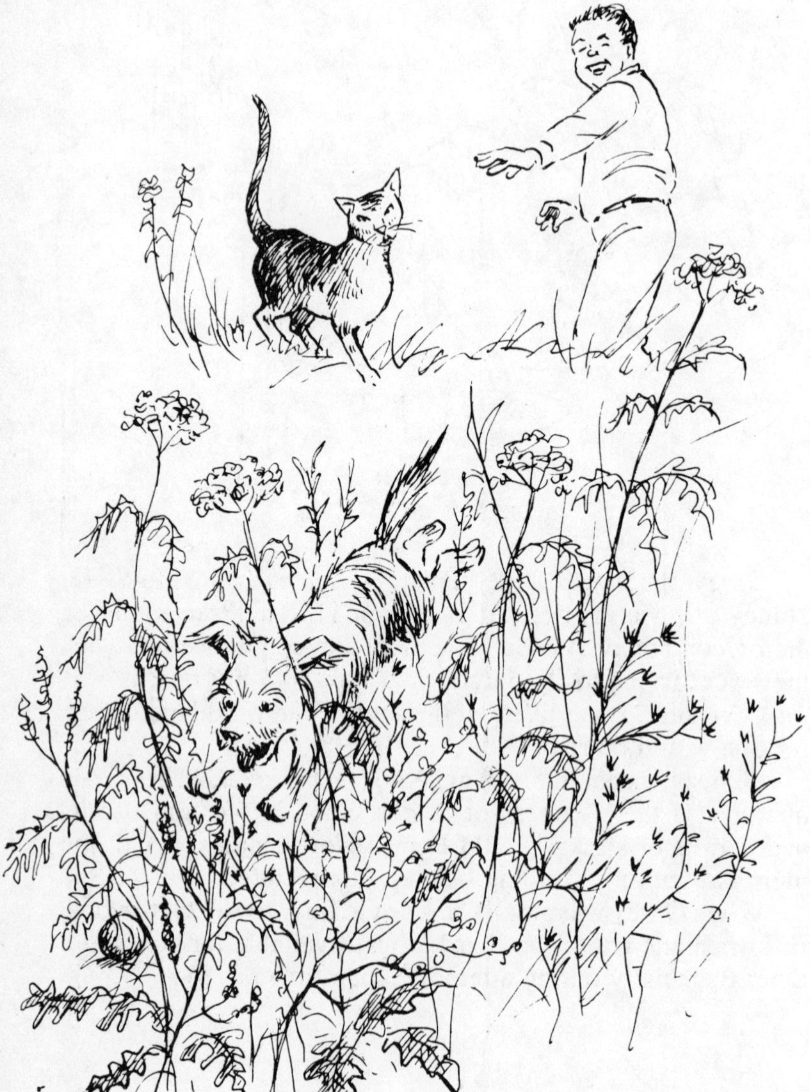

Teaching humans to respond to simple signals or commands is important. Your tail is very helpful in this matter. You should always use your tail dramatically and with dignity. Remember this may be the only indication your human may have for guessing what you are thinking.

This does not mean wagging. Dogs wag their tails and smile till their silly tongues hang out. What does it get them? They have to learn senseless tricks to show how clever their human is. They rush off into the weeds to find balls and squeeky toys, and just when they get back exhausted and full of fresh fleas, the human chunks the ball into another weed patch and screams "Fetch."

Cats do not fetch. Not papers, or slippers or squeeky toys. They may occasionally bring you something, such as a dead animal. But this is on a purely voluntary basis.

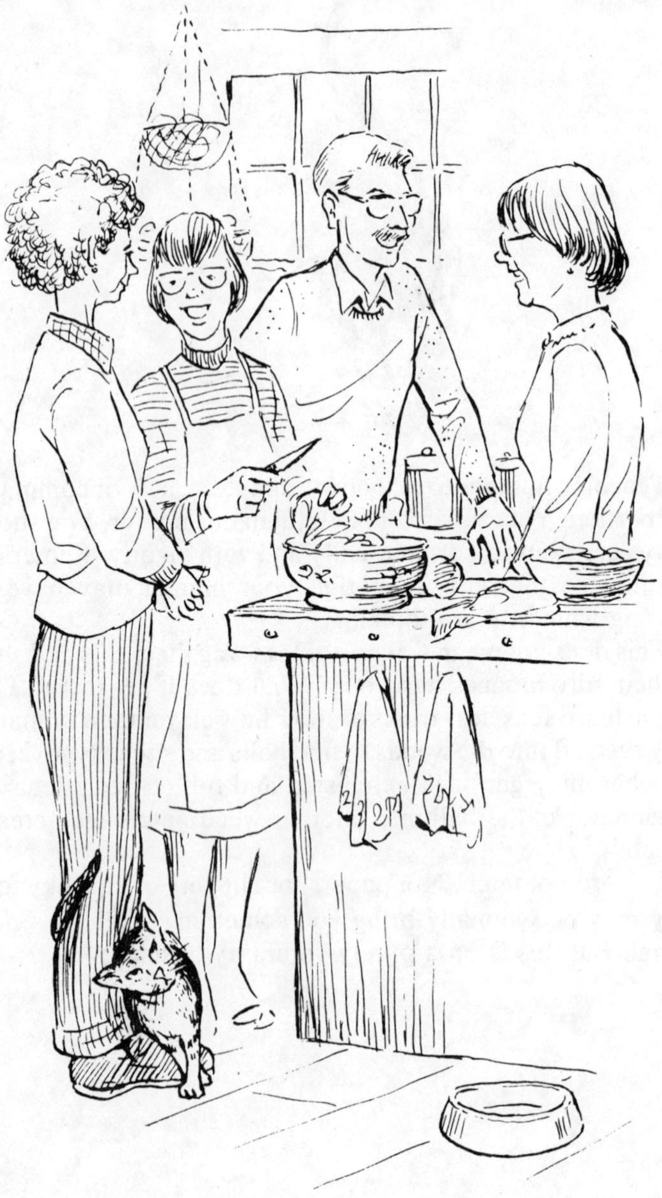

A smart cat, however, can teach a human to fetch any number of things. Food, water, fresh pine-scented litter, and an occasional catnip toy. They will also learn to open doors and windows on command. It is really a matter of getting their attention.

When you have a pressing need, such as lunch, the act of weaving in and out of a female human's legs will often make them aware of your desire. If this does not bring an almost immediate response, you can try throwing your normally beautiful voice slightly out of gear and the sound will turn into a rasping note that sends chills through the most solidly built human. Repeated often, and with a certain insistence — which is somewhere between a polite request and a demand — this music will usually bring even the most distracted human to your attention.

In no time they will be asking you what you want and hurrying to find the solution so you will stop calling. I myself have brought the conversation of a kitchen full of chatty humans to a dead halt with just the right note in my voice.

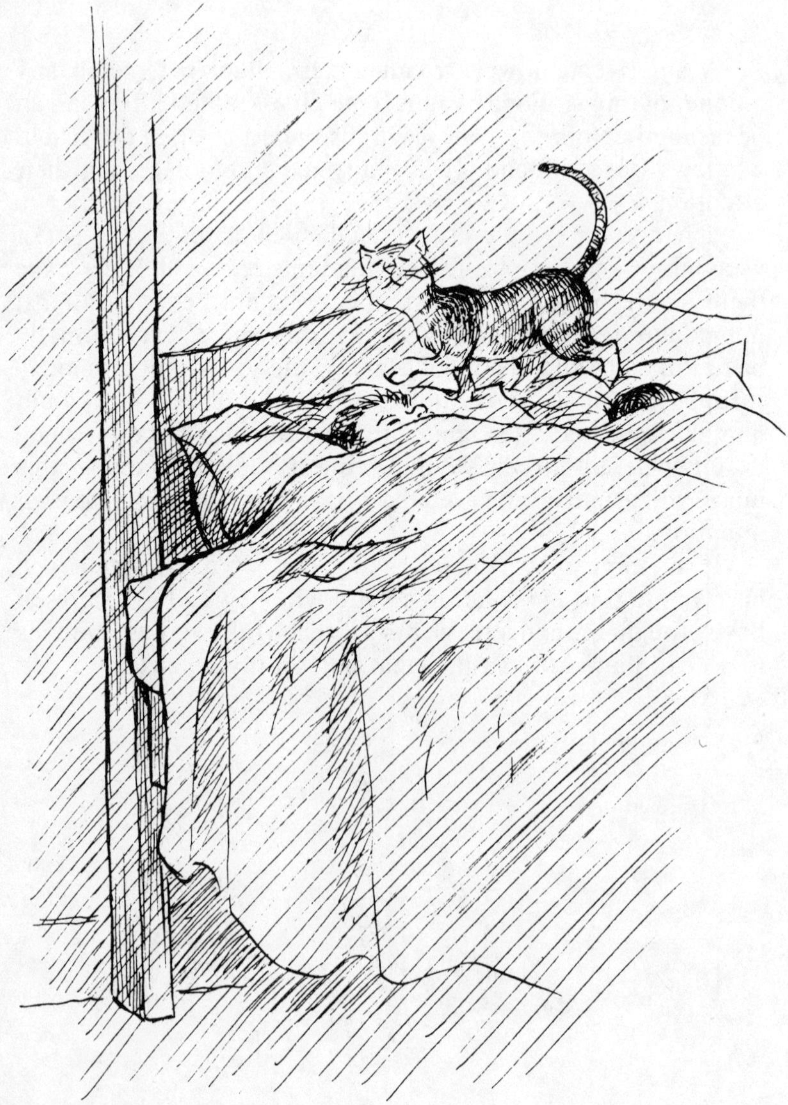

During the dark hours it is sometimes necessary to use additional actions to get fed or have a door opened so you can go for a moonlit roam. Humans sleep rather soundly and tend to bury themselves in pillows and various materials so that a normal mew doesn't always penetrate their brain. At this point it becomes necessary to resort to physical contact to bring them into action.

Two techniques have worked quite well for me in the past. One is to saunter across the top of the bed just above the pillow line. As I move along I find occasion to drag my midsection or tail across the head of the sleeper. About the third trip across I may put a clumsy paw on the forehead or nose of my benefactor.

When doing this it is necessary to be ready to move quickly to avoid flying arms. Male humans seem to resent this approach and will lash out wildly.

My Sweet Nancy and Carey, being more gentle and refined, will respond graciously and drag themselves from under the covers to take care of my needs. Unfortunately, Sweet Nancy, having a pure heart, sleeps sounder than Old Paint so I have had to be constantly on the alert for attack.

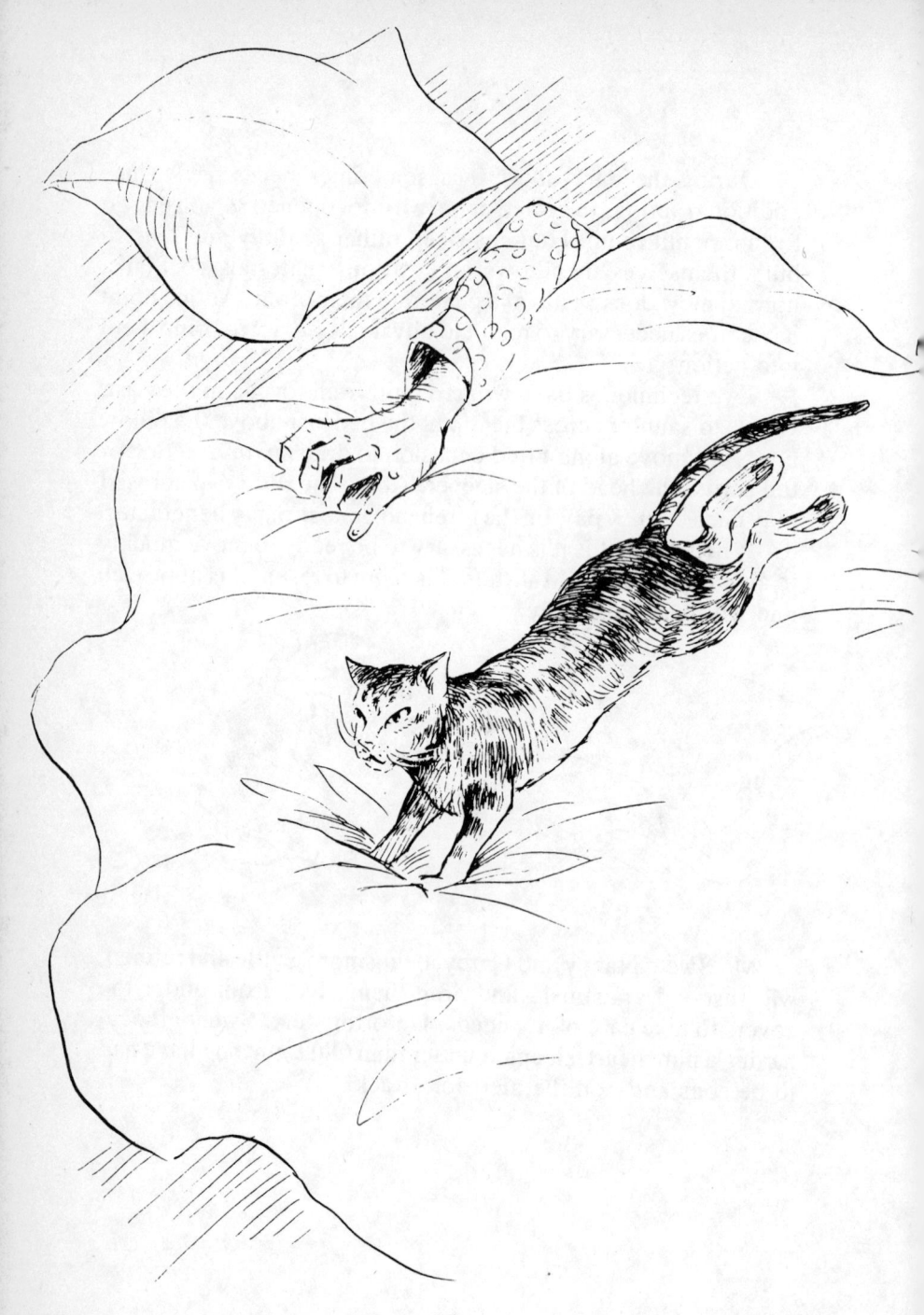

A safer method of getting attention is to do a head-to-foot gallop across the bed, landing as hard as you can on all of the lumpy areas that present themselves. A diagonal path is the safest route — such as his-head-to-her-feet. This gets a lot of reaction. The first person you hit will usually bound up in confusion waking the other person.

Moving diagonally also confuses the sleepers and the male is likely to throw pillows in the wrong direction or fall out of bed.

Be wary of waking the wrong one first. In my youth I made the mistake several times of rushing from her-feet-to-his-head. This landed me right in the clutches of the wrong party and I found myself bouncing off the far wall.

If you are the sort of cat who fancies a heating pad in the winter you may desire to risk the dangers of sleeping in a human bed. Some humans take naturally to this and make wonderful nighttime pets.

Older humans do not rest as soundly and tend to fidget while you are making your preliminary stroll around the bed covers to find just the right spot. Then, of course, no resting place is fit to settle in until it has been "claw-danced" for a little while. You should avoid doing this near the head of the bed.

Given my choice I would sleep on top of the large middle part of the human's body. This is the warmest area. For some reason this causes them to thrash about, which makes rest uncertain. Once I settle down I do not want my nest to behave like a water bed. Then, too, there are the rumblings and gurgles that go on some nights. This can be very distracting.

The best location then, is to locate yourself quietly between the human's legs. This pins them to the bed and often forces them to spend the night unwittingly locked in this position.

Under-the-covers-sleeping should only be done with perfectly trained humans. For myself I prefer to be out in the open in case of attack instead of trapped under a lot of blankets.

Now I suppose I should try and tell you more about how to train the human male. This is an almost impossible task. If you have the choice, the simplest solution would be to choose only female humans for pets. There are many types to choose among and most of them, being sensitive and almost catlike in their thinking, will make excellent pets.

Very old female humans make wonderful companions. They love to sit in the sun for long periods of time reading or sewing things for small humans who are nowhere to be seen. They also have similar tastes in food to cats and often cater to things we find especially nice. They are genuinely appreciative of a good purr and always seem ready to turn their attention from TV to let us out of the door.

Unfortunately they don't live as long as cats do. Occasionally at the prime of life you may find yourself living with a house full of those screaming little humans who received all of the sewing gifts.

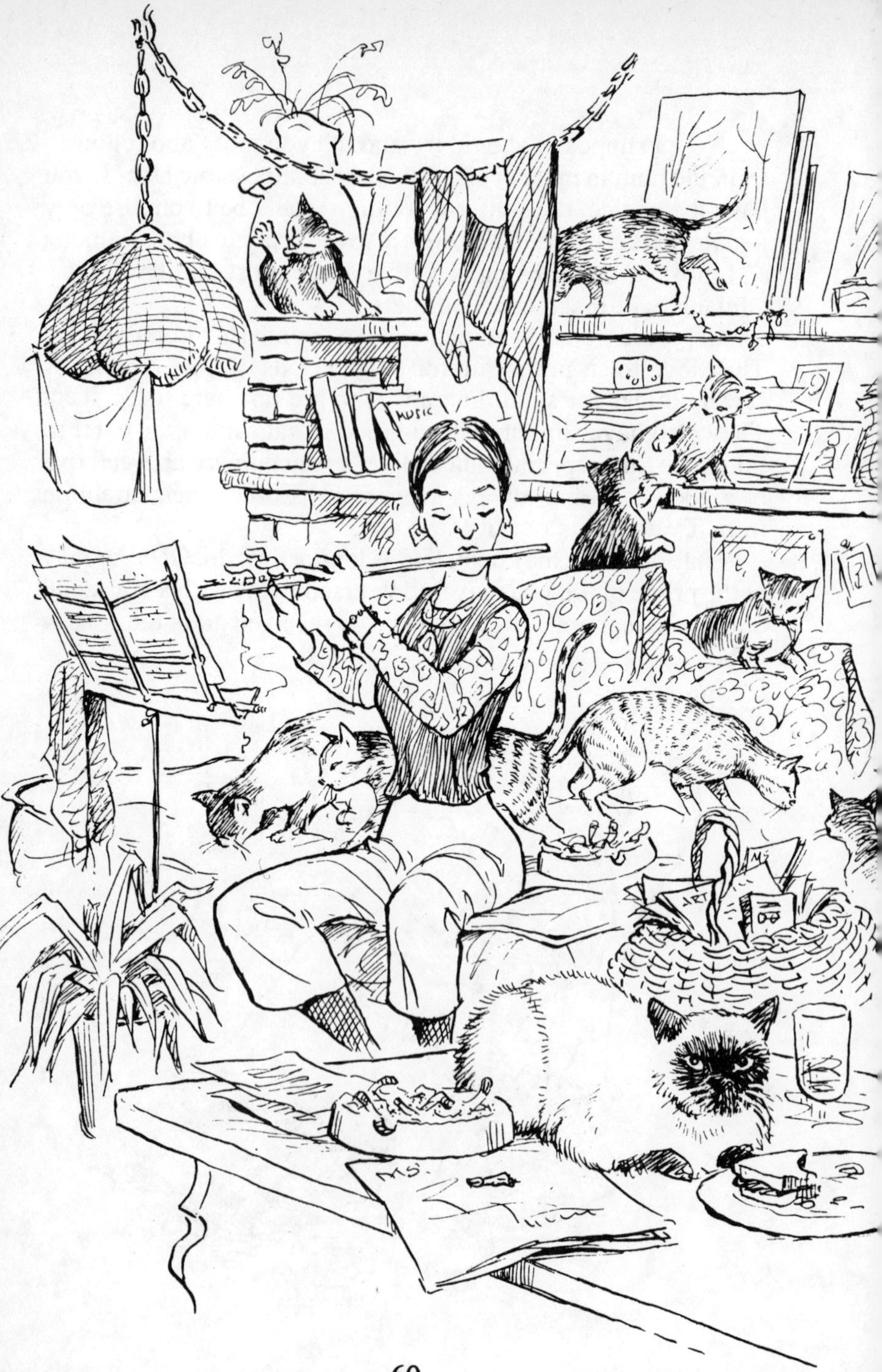
MUSIC
ART
MS
MS.

Sometimes you can adopt a pair of females in the same house. They often show you a great deal of attention. The one difficulty with this situation is that there seems to be no end of cats who decide to adopt this twosome. In time the house will become filled with competition, so that you must line up to be petted or fed.

Single female humans who are not yet old are also available. They are nice but less desirable. They are gone from the house most of the day working at something. When they do come home there is often a parade of males who show up. This is somewhat like tom-catting as we know it, although the males do not spend as much time growling and fighting with each other in the alley. The males have very little use for us cats. Since there are always different males coming, there is no time to train them. They all look alike although some of them smell better than others. In the end the female human often mates with one of the males and then there are human kittens.

So there you are back in the first situation again.

On the bright side most males are out of the house all day. When they do come in they often go to the basement or outside to scratch in the ground. I don't think this has anything to do with litter box training.

What they do is annoy bushes and flowers with their clipping and pulling. I have sat for hours in a clump of day lilies watching Old Paint snatch and pull perfectly good crab grass out of the earth and throw it away.

Males also like to eat. This they do to excess. Sweet Nancy and my girls are hard put to keep enough food on the table to satisfy Old Paint. In addition, the girls are always leaving a lot of little delights on their plates for me, whereas old vacuum mouth would eat the design off the surface if he could get it loose.

At night, after they have eaten, most males do one of several things. They sit and watch TV — they sit and go to sleep — they go back to banging in the basement — or they leave the house again, sometimes taking the big female with them. In any of these cases the best course is to keep a low profile until they settle down. Then the house is yours to run again with your more obedient pets.

I almost wish I didn't have to mention the small male human pet.
It is called the Boy.

I have never had any of them for long in my house. My strongest advice is to avoid adopting any. I have it on good authority that they are totally untrainable. They are very loud and physical. No cat is safe in their path. The best thing to do is sic the dog on them. Dogs love the sort of banging around boys give them. I personally can't imagine being wrestled and rolled on. But dogs will be dogs, and they deserve each other.

I had lived for some years adjusted to what they call city life. I found enough action fighting with the Toms in the neighborhood to keep my blood up and acquire some interesting scars and a rather ragged left ear. I learned about cars by being slightly squashed by one in my youth. The girls in my home settled down in a few years to a pattern of going away part of the day so I could have a morning nap while Sweet Nancy talked to the box on the wall to keep it company.

In the afternoon the girls came home and played with each other or their other human friends. Then they sat and did what they called lessons. Kathleen would stand on her head for a while, and Meg would create houses under tables. Carey spent a lot of time rearranging her room.

Each year when the days got long and warm, suddenly everyone would begin to stack up the things they liked best and close the windows and doors. One day I would be scooped up and put in the car along with all of the collected treasures. The rest of my pets would climb in and scream, "Goodbye," to all of the neighbors.

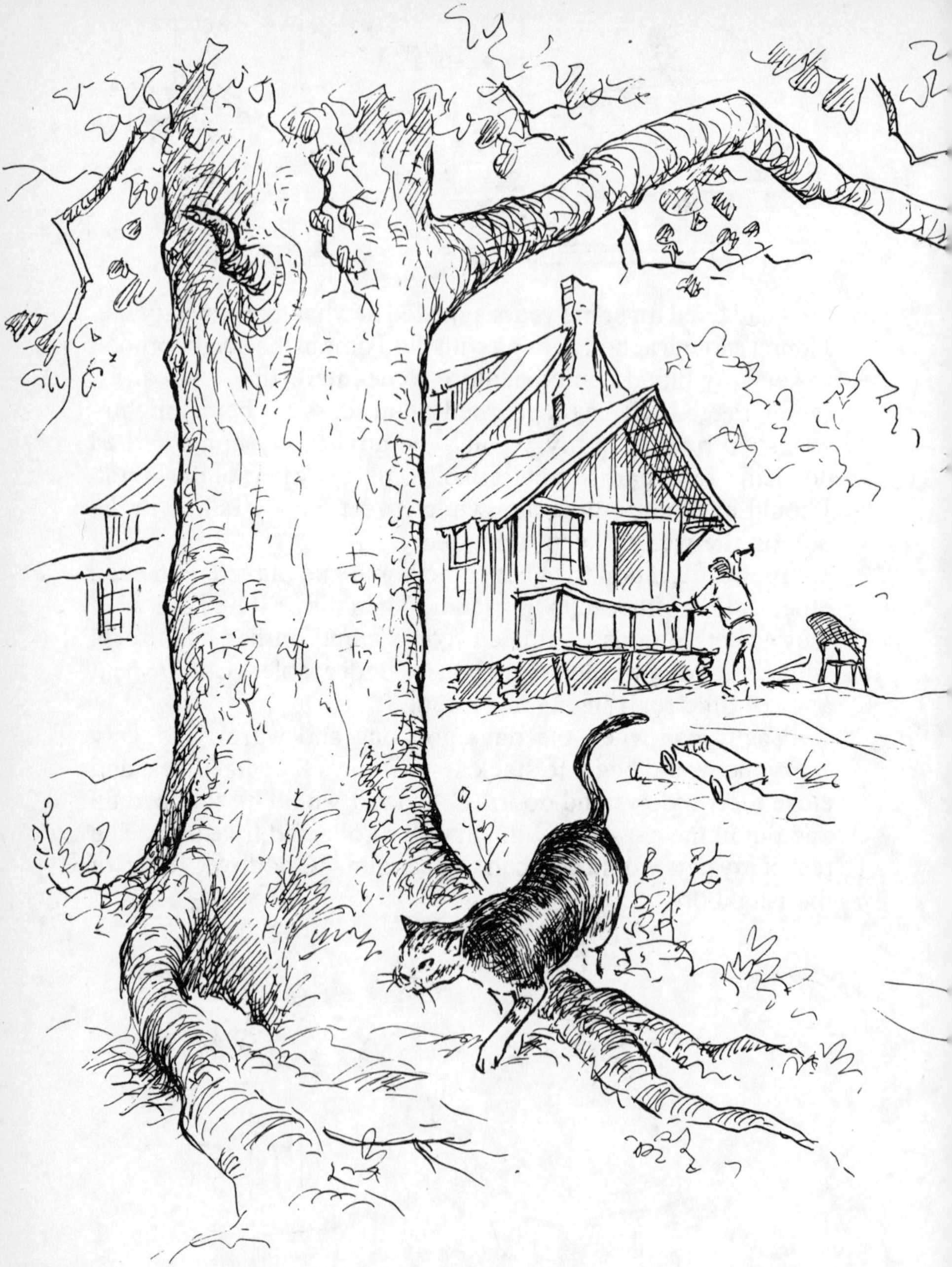

After rumbling along for a great time we would arrive at the little tumbled-down house where I had first adopted the family. Then for the long days that followed I would enjoy living much as I had in my youth. There would be trees and barns and lots and lots of wild life to stalk.

The humans would be busy doing their usual senseless activities. I used to think how nice it was that I had even trained them to take me back to the scenes of my youth for a little change.

Old Paint was forever banging and tearing at the little house but I accepted this as a harmless amusement.

All during the warm time other humans would come and sleep and eat in the tumbled-down house. They all seemed to enjoy each other. There would be lots of small humans, too. They would bunch up with my girls and play chase-your-tail games in the grass. They also loved to dress up in strange clothes. Fortunately they no longer involved me in this activity.

Sometimes there would be small male humans in the group. I gave them a wide berth. They did all of the things that I had heard about them doing, including climbing up in trees and falling out. They did not land in sensible catlike ways, but crashed on their heads or limbs with great howling noises. After that they would lie around much quieter or hop and stagger for the rest of their visit.

Each year when the weather got cooler we would go through the same packing up and rumbling off to the nice warm city house. This always reminded me of the last time I saw Mumz in her wicker basket. Of course there was none of the dignity of her departure in our move.

The girls would be laughing and screaming. Old Paint would fuss and fume about what was left and how I should not be on top of what he called his "art." Only Sweet Nancy kept things moving along and occasionally even she would dissolve into tears over the confusion. The safest place for me to be was as close to Carey as possible.

"Cricket needs more room to lie down," she would say in a loud voice over the confusion.

I will not record what Old Paint often replied. Besides, even he would not do things like that to anyone.

Then Carey would somehow make enough room for me to lie down anyway, even if it meant talking Kathleen into sitting on the floorboards.

Now I must admit this change of scenery every year was a pleasure to me. It also gave me a certain prestige with the cats in the city neighborhood. Very few of them had their humans so well trained that they would go to such lengths to let their cat hunt field mice.

It never occurred to me that these pleasant summer sojourns would ever take on any more significance than a temporary change of pace. Like going to the store for cat food or to the Vet for a shot. When it came to serious living — especially when it got cold — the only place to be was in that warm city house.

Then suddenly things changed. One year we went to the country the same as usual and didn't come back.

If I had known what was happening I might have tried to stop them. I had done it before on a temporary basis. If I did not want to leave I would disappear just as everything was packed. Then there would be frantic searching and calling in the neighborhood.

This was only a delaying action which could, at best, last a matter of hours. How I might have been able to prevent the finality of this move I have never been able to decide.

I soon found out that the cause of the upheaval had something to do with Old Paint.

Humans kept saying to him "So, now you are a Fine Artist, eh?"

I saw nothing fine about him. He was as rumpled as ever and to make matters worse he was always around. He did stay in one of the little sheds a lot of the time throwing colors at bits of paper, but I could never tell when he was going to come lumbering in to feed his face with tuna fish salad or make coffee.

I shuddered at the thought of staying in that drafty shack in the cold winter. I also wondered whether my pets would behave all year around as they had on our summer visits.

In the past they had performed in strange ways. They wore less coverings on their funny shapes. They built fires in the yard at night and threw perfectly good food in the middle until it was almost burnt to a crisp. Then they would make loud noises about how good it was to eat. They would go off in the woods and pull up weeds to bring in the house to make each other sneeze. They splashed in the little pond near the house and tried to entice us animals to do it too. I had more sense, but there was an old dog called Ignatz who would put up with this madness in the name of friendship.

To avoid all of this I spent a lot of time on the metal roof where there was a bit of shade and the breeze could rumple my fur.

Now, I had to face the reality of this major change. And since it might come to your world too, I will attempt to tell you a little about what to expect.

Humans in the woods are different. First, I suppose, there is the house. Perhaps some humans find decent buildings when they move.

We did Not.

This place leaked cold air at every window and door. Only a few rooms were ever heated when the humans were awake — and never at night.

As the first cold weather approached I began a frantic search for a draft-free place to curl up. The humans kept talking about "quaint and charming" when they showed strange visitors around. There is nothing quaint about a cold breeze up your backside.

Old Paint kept banging at the walls and moving doors and windows around when he wasn't throwing paint on paper. It did no good. The cracks just got rearranged.

In the end, the changes only confused the strangers who kept coming to live with us for a few days. They would wander in the halls with their toothbrushes calling to each other about where the bathroom had gone.

This is another thing about humans in the woods. There is a never ending parade of new humans moving in and out all of the time. I was kept busy trying to make judgements on whether to let them pick me up or not.

It would not be right to pass off all of them as hostile. I met one, in my more mature years, named Gretel who knew just how to scratch my back so that I tingled right down to the tips of my paws and tail. Apparently she had been well trained in her youth by some wise cat. Just thinking about her fingers makes my whiskers twitch.

In general it is always best to keep your distance until you know what to expect from strangers.

In the cold weather there are fewer of them, but when they do come, the house is a lot warmer. Old Paint seems to regard the comforts of humans more than he does cats. He will build fires in rooms that usually stay cold as outdoors. Suddenly I am overrun with wonderful snug places to sleep.

If I sense that a new visitor is catwise, I always seek her out. This often leads to a warm lap and a good rub. I also make note of which room she is nesting in since she might want company at night in a strange house.

I met an English lady human called Sheila, one very cold winter, who seemed to need a friend. At bedtime Old Paint told her that she should keep her door closed or "that cat" would come visiting. This was certainly true, but rather unkindly put since the lady had obviously taken a strong fancy to me. She did as she was told and there I was left in the dining room as the old house began to chill over.

Finally I took matters into my own paws and, backing the length of the room, I ran full force and flung myself at the guest room door. It came open with a crash and in a wisk I was in the kind lady's bed. When she stopped screaming she seemed very happy to have me join her and we settled down for a very satisfactory sleep.

Now, not all humans are as receptive. There is one female called Nana who loves warmth as much as I do, but she won't share it with me. She comes quite often and when she does the house is especially warm. Wonder of wonders, Old Paint even puts heat in her bedroom.

But do you think she will share it? Not on your flea collar. She even keeps the door closed during the day.

On top of that she is always making wild noises about me resting on the kitchen counters, and slapping her hands together to frighten me off.

I have great patience, as we cats must have when dealing with humans. They don't all respond to training as quickly as they should. For years I have been working on this Nana human to get her to let me share that warm bedroom.

Whenever she sits down in the TV room I always wander onto her lap and try to show her how very desirable I am. She has a very large warm lap and I like to sit in it. She still resists and keeps saying, "Why does this cat like me so much?"

This is a strange reaction. Then she keeps pushing me off on to the floor. But I know the only way to make humans learn is to keep repeating the action until they catch on.

Always remember, with enough patience, you-*can*-teach-an-old-human-new-tricks.

I think I have said enough about this old house. I have spent ten cold, damp, snowy seasons in it, and if I walk a bit crooked and don't pounce as well as I did, you can put it down to cold nights in a lonely basket.

Humans in the woods develop another trait that is perhaps the most disrupting when one is trying to run a well ordered home.

In the city I reigned supreme as master of my human pets. In the woods they immediately began littering my world with other animals. Perhaps they thought that since they had visitors coming and going that I wanted companions too.

I was never consulted on this matter.

Soon after we arrived in the woods the old dog Ignatz went away.

"Good," thought I.

Then the humans had a big party on the lawn with more other humans than I ever want to see again. They seemed to favor two of the group more than each other. They were dressed in city garments and everyone threw rice at them. When the couple tried to get away, they chased the car and threw more rice.

Among the milling humans who kept hugging each other and crying were a lot of dogs who had come along, I suppose, to cheer them up. At the end of the day all of the strangers got in their cars and roared off — dogs and all.

All but one.

This one came bouncing into the house and began jumping up in peoples' lap and making disgusting lapping noises, as if she were trying to wash every human in sight.

The next thing I knew this straggly-haired twitch was bedding down on the porch and making advances on my dinner bowl. Her name was Ms. Wiggles and this certainly fit her.

Then in no time Old Paint came in with another dog called Frolich. This, I understand, means "Joyful" in some other human language.

She was not Joyful, which shows that dogs are not good at languages. Her only trick seemed to be rolling over on her back and sticking her feet in the air whenever anyone said anything nice to her.

Now dogs have their place. Fortunately this is limited to the floor and certain low items like chairs and sofas. They do not have the talent for climbing trees or leaping gracefully from table top to pantry shelf. This gave me a lot of room to avoid any contact with the new invaders.

But then Carey caught on to the strange new trend of collecting, and suddenly one day a tiny kitten appeared in her room.

At first I thought it was a fuzzy mouse — but not so. I also hoped that it might fall into one of the holes that Old Paint had failed to patch and disappear forever. Again disappointment.

Carey was very protective of the new thing which she called Boofer. All I could think of at that point was maybe Cricket wasn't such a bad name after all.

Soon Boofer began to make trips into the rest of the house and finally into my sacred areas — dinner bowls, sunny window ledges and even Sweet Nancy's lap. I knocked her cocksided several times, but cats don't threaten as well as dogs do. She came bouncing back wanting to play with my tail.

Now I was at that time a cat of many years dignity. No one, human or otherwise, had played with my tail since I was a kit. It had been pulled a few times by Meg and her friends, but they had soon learned that the claw-is-quicker-than-the-eye.

Two cats in a house make for a divided kingdom. Disciplining humans is hard enough, but when you have more than one cat laying down rules the humans get confused and unmanageable. They also tend to favor the little kittens because they spend so much time bouncing about. This pleases humans because they are very easily entertained.

I was not about to compete with such foolishness. I took to the rooftop and spent the summer sunning and sulking.

Meanwhile, Boofer grew into a cat. This was some relief. She was not a particularly good looking feline, being a mixture of grey, black and white spots all in the wrong places. I am sure she didn't have a drop of Persian in her.

Then she took to wandering in the moonlight.

A smart human would have known what to do about that. They certainly did in my case. I think Old Paint was getting soft in his old age about having little things around.

Sure enough in the spring Boofer gave him a cardboard box full of kittens.

They were everywhere in no time. Boofer would gather them in the garden and teach them to stalk. I had visions of my hunting grounds being depleted.

Then just as I began to despair, the kittens began to disappear. Smiling strangers came and scooped them up and went away. I began sitting on the fence to watch for the next car coming down the road.

But they stopped coming before the last kitten disappeared. Now there was this fat striped male called Hawthorne in my world.

It wasn't long before he went for a ride to visit the Vet. When he came back, Hawthorne seemed content to just lounge around. Except for collecting an occasional mouse he has spent his life strolling from lap to lap and eating.

The next one to bring in a stranger was my own Sweet Nancy. Once she began, there seemed to be no discrimination in her choices.

One time it was a day-old chicken called Peep.

It took up residence in a bedroom off the kitchen. All day long it kept calling its own name. I found this the height of conceit. No one ever saw me going around saying "Cricket" all day. I might have been inclined to say "Lawrence" occasionally if things had been otherwise, but hardly "Cricket."

For some reason Ms. Wiggles decided that Peep was her long lost child. She would stand at the closed door all day, fidgeting nervously as Peep continued to peep. When anyone went in the room, the silly dog would dash in as if preparing to do whatever motherlike thing she could to help out. Mostly this consisted of sitting and watching intently as Peep danced around pecking at dust balls and occasionally Ms. Wiggles' nose.

Peep soon began to ride around on Sweet Nancy's shoulder as she did her chores. She would rush from one shoulder blade to the other keeping a keen eye out for what was going on below. Sweet Nancy soon began to walk with a crouch so Peep's perch would be more level. I feel sure if Peep had grown to full chickenhood that Sweet Nancy would have developed into a bent human to keep that fowl happy. Mercifully, one sunny day Peep was given the run of the vegetable garden and disappeared under mysterious circumstances.

Undismayed, Sweet Nancy next arrived home with a large full-grown buck rabbit called Buck.

A cage was built and Buck sat for a year and ate anything put before him, while small visiting humans came and went to look at the "big bunny."

One day Sweet Nancy decided that Buck was so tame and lovable that she would give him a little romp in the grass before his bed time.

We never saw him again.

Somewhere along, one of the many humans who came and went presented Carey with yet another kitten, just when I was beginning to knock Boofer and Hawthorne into shape.

This one was called Edith.

At first I had hopes of her being stepped on in the dinner hour rush, because she was always underfoot. She also had the habit of scurrying wildly up the side of any human who stood still. This often led to shrieks of pain and surprise from unsuspecting visitors who weren't accustomed to being substituted for a maple tree. Once Edith had successfully reached the shoulders of her human perch she would cling desperately to cloth and flesh until she found the next place to jump.

I took myself back to the secluded heights of the roof to sun and sulk.

Once again the Vet visit was delayed and there was a box of kittens in the spring. As luck would have it, all but one disappeared down the road.

There remained a slight creature called Gwenevere.

Unlike the fat Hawthorne she has remained small and very female. I must admit she even has a bit of culture in her looks. Her face *is* quite Egyptian. Her father had been a large cat with bright green eyes. His name was Mr. Grey and he spent several weeks sitting on a bale of hay by the chicken house waiting for the erratic Edith to choose her moments to go courting.

With the coming of Gwenevere, even Sweet Nancy decided that the house was getting too full for any more residents. Gwenevere made a visit to the Vet early in her life and never found any gentlemen friends on the fence.

This was not the last of the adoptions, however.

There remained Chuck Duck to crowd my world.

Chuck had been one of those badly colored animals who arrive in time for Easter and live a short and decorative life at the mercy of small humans who quickly love them to death.

Somehow Chuck had escaped this fate and when Sweet Nancy appeared at the door with him he had been washed clean of his Easter finery and was a bright yellow once more.

Chuck became a close friend of Meg who had recently lost a turtle named Charlie Blossom. A large box in her room became Chuck's home and we seldom saw him in the general confusion of the kitchen where the rest of us animals helped Sweet Nancy prepare our food.

In the spring Chuck could be seen sitting on Meg's stomach as she lay in the grass studying her lessons. He never felt close to anyone else, but his devotion to Meg was almost doglike in its intensity.

One day in summer when Chuck had grown full size and gone all white, Meg took him to the pond at the foot of the hill and set him free. Chuck circled out into the big water and came back to be fed. For several days Chuck and Meg kept up a quacking-calling conversation from house to pond.

All seemed well. We were rid of one resident. Then a mud turtle bit Chuck, and he had to go to the Vet for repairs. He came back with one less leg.

Now ducks, as we know, are not graceful on land. We cats make a ballet out of stalking a lizard. The duck can only pounce and gobble. Waddle is a duck term. Fat humans and ducks waddle.

Chuck did less than that. He stumbled and floundered. Finally he discovered that he could manage a strange lopsided hop. Before he could work on this much, Meg appeared with a large plastic pool.

Chuck spent the summer in luxury, being fed by every small human who came on the place. Bugs, grasshoppers, ants and even small fish caught in the pond, he attacked everything with the same vigor. In return he grew very fat and quacked a lot.

When cold weather came Chuck was moved into the greenhouse which had become part of the winter sitting room.

Old Paint, in his never ending banging on the house, had lumped together the few areas he decided were worthy of heat, and it is here that we animals found some comfort.

Chuck sat on a nest of fresh straw under the steps and watched the flies in the window all day. Occasionally he would let out a loud burst of quacks and flop his wings around for exercise. This always got a reaction out of unsuspecting houseguests.

Then Chuck began to leave eggs around. This seemed hardly a "Chuck" thing to do. It was too late to change the name to Chuckette or Chuckeriene or something worse. This was fortunate. It was also good that Chuck had no motherly feeling for the eggs. They went for breakfast and nothing was ever said about having little ducklings.

Chuck lived a well tended life, winter and summer, until she laid her last egg in the garden and passed on during her third year.

The point of all of this, kitties, is that humans are very unpredictable. Their affections are uncertain. They already had the best of all household companions and they chose to go berserk with the riff-raff of the animal kingdom.

It would be pointless to dwell at length on the outdoor menagerie. The house was surrounded by cows who bellowed constantly to be fed. In the garden a shed full of chickens squabbled and bragged about what they had accomplished in the nesting boxes. When Sweet Nancy wasn't carrying scraps to the hen house, she was chasing cows back into their pasture. Old Paint is as good at building fences as he is at fixing cold air cracks. Suddenly, the yard would be full of cows, calves and humans. The humans would all be yelling in what they assumed to be cow language. The cows would be darting between the barns and bee hives in a mixture of defiance and confusion.

It is at such times that I feel it is a good thing to remind the humans that you, the cat, are at least performing a valuable service by being around.

I find that an occasional mouse or shrew dropped in the middle of the kitchen floor is a good way to emphasize this importance.

The young cats, particularly Boofer, like to chew parts of their prey and leave little bits of this and that around.

I personally think this very untidy.

Hawthorne, on the other hand, likes to play with his catch.

This has a very bad effect on humans, particularly during the preparation of a meal. A dazed mouse staggering about between the feet of Sweet Nancy and the girls has a negative effect on my getting tasty nibbles during the pre-dinner time.

Guests have an even more disturbed reaction which sometimes involves shrieking and throwing things, as well as running wildly out of the room. One female bolted out the door at Thanksgiving and locked herself in the car. It was necessary to pass little helpings of turkey and stuffing through the window of her Dodge to keep her alive until she could return to the city.

As I have said, a whole mouse — quite dead — is your best calling card.

* * *

There is not much more advice I can give to you cats of tomorrow. I have seen a lot of weather and mice and moles in my time. I don't seem to get much out of hunting any more. The mice are faster now than when I was young. I give a fair show of wandering around in the garden giving off angry "Rowwws" at what might be something in the leaves. But I really prefer to lie in the sun on a warm sofa or in the middle of the pot plants that line the greenhouse shelves.

Mostly I watch.

I watch the family I have always known and see them change. The girls are as big as Sweet Nancy now. I am glad they aren't as rumpled as Old Paint. They all work in the kitchen or garden doing things that humans seem to find necessary.

Carey has moved out into a little room over the root cellar. Her house is almost hidden by the highbush blueberries. Here a cat or dog is really made welcome. There is always room in her bed for one more on a cold night.

She organized us into a hiking society a few years ago. In the afternoons we would troop off across the pasture and into the woods to see what leaves had fallen and where the new spider webs were spun. Our procession usually wound up a little ragged. The dogs always wanted to pick up sticks and rush off as if someone up ahead were asking them to fetch. In the rear the smaller cats would drag behind and stop to rest too often. In the end Carey would wind up carrying one or more back to the house. I always managed to keep a steady pace until the year my back end began to get creaky.

I notice the girls go away for long periods of time now and come back full of chatter about things that have no meaning to me.

I have found a shelf in the kitchen that I can still get up on, if I jump carefully. I like to climb up there where I can look out at all of the goings on without getting stepped on. Sweet Nancy has cleared a bit of the china away so that I can lie comfortably without having to push some of the things off on the floor.

Getting up on things is not what it once was. I have to take a long run and do a lot of scrambling to climb up on the perch where we cats feed. Some times even Old Paint will give me a lift up when he sees I am not going to make it. I think he is going soft.

Perhaps I am getting mellow too. However, as long as I can fix a hard stare on anyone who tries to bother me, I think they will believe I am still fierce.

I think, after all is said, that I have done a pretty good job of training my human pets — even here in the woods. Carey, in particular, would make any cat happy to own her.

This winter has been very nice, because all of the girls have been at home. When the cold drafts come creeping through the cracks it is good to have the room with the TV full of people. There is such a good selection of warm laps to choose among, that even if some of the faster cats like Gwenevere get first choice, there is still enough to go around. Then with the wind howling around the outside we sit, cats, dogs and humans, and have a long evening of each other and the snug feeling that only this kind of time can give you.

I do not like to think now of a time when there will not be enough laps to go around. The room will seem cold even with the heater going.

Soon spring will be here and I will make my way slowly to the sunshine spots that I still fancy.

Right now I just like to watch and enjoy these moments.

I would be the last to give up my independence as a cat. A cat should always belong to himself. Sentimentality is for dogs and humans. However, dear future cats, I must admit that there is something good about having human pets.

And for every Old Paint there will probably be three nice girls. And maybe, if you are very, very lucky, there will be a Sweet Nancy.

Just remember, to always think Persian.

Yours, once and for all,
a cat named Cricket

* * *

Cricket did not have to face a time of dwindling laps. The spring of his seventeenth year came and he did indeed find his place in the sunshine for a little while.

Then in May, when the best of springtime had arrived and our little valley was bursting with flowers and new life, he developed a tumor. The girls took him to the Vet, but it was too late.

They brought him carefully home in a small box and we laid him to rest below the well house in the shade of a clump of maples overlooking the pond. Next to him is Chuck Duck and other animal friends who have come and gone.

Meg said once, just after Chuck was hurt, that everything she loved seemed to die. I fear this is the way of life.

But perhaps by recording the ramblings of this' fierce, grouchy, dear old alley cat he can live on a while longer in our memories and we will learn to value the opportunity to share our laps with other animals yet to come.

John Kollock
(Old Paint)

Cricket was a real cat. For 17 years he ruled his household with an iron paw. There has been some discussion about who really wrote this book. It is true that John Kollock pecked out the words on his ancient typewriter, but the sentiment and thinking is pure Cricket — as anyone who knew him will testify.

John Kollock is a real artist. He has written articles and books on the subjects close to him for years. THESE GENTLE HILLS and THE LONG AFTERNOON deal with the history and rural life of the Georgia mountains he grew up in. MEG'S WORLD, now in its third printing, is about the world of his children. John has illustrated some 25 other books. His watercolor paintings are in many public and private collections, including a former President and several Governors.

He does live in a very tumbled-down old farm house in the mountains with his wife Nancy and family. Here, in spite of cold weather and bad heating, he manages to do his art work and writing.